FINISHING LINE PRESS

www.finishinglinepress.com

the loneliness
of a planet without a moon

a poem in a matter of days

by

Kathleen Jesme

Finishing Line Press
Georgetown, Kentucky

the loneliness
of a planet without a moon

a poem in a matter of days

ACKNOWLEDGMENTS

To those who read this work in its making and reflected on it, gratitude:

Christin Lore-Weber, Francine Sterle, Amy McNamara, Anna Meek, Katrina
Vandenberg, Eleanor Wilner, Judith Savage, Alaina Hagen.

Publisher: Leah Huete de Maines
Editor: Christen Kincaid
Cover Art: Kathleen Walsh
Author Photo: Alaina Hagen/Medbh McNamara
Cover Design: Elizabeth Maines McCleavy

Order online: www.finishinglinepress.com
also available on amazon.com

Author inquiries and mail orders:
Finishing Line Press
PO Box 1626
Georgetown, Kentucky 40324
USA

Distance is
Until thyself, Beloved.

—Dickinson

Day 4

Before the white season   when it should have come   or shall come
before the time when the moon goes down just   as the sun rises
and the air is still and cool   not like winter air   but also not like fall
when hanging from the trees a few crisp blood-dried leaves   hold their place
the train approaches the crossing   sends its long hollow call
a late robin wanders the dormant grass   kicking up a bit of fuss

And I think of you then   of the gap   between us   not a chasm
exactly but more than a doorway   and more than the years   that have passed us
and sure enough the snow begins   drops its mask   on the present
and what came before   so that I am no longer waiting   no longer
hoping for anything   nor stilled   by the distance

*

As if a hole had appeared
out of nowhere
the day
did not exist

I had to learn
to interrogate my own bones
the edifice of my body to look
for gaps and missing sectors

I had to learn
to find the stones
of me

I had to believe in
getting lost

Day 11

In the dusk   a young buck deer came to the sunflower feeder   and ate almost
daintily taking each mouthful   and looking around
to see what dangers might rise   out of the surrounding

We turned out   the lights to become invisible   but I knew the deer
could hear us whispering   could feel us watching   could perhaps
even smell us being there   in the darkened house   marveling
at how young he was   how petite   probably a yearling
with a small neat rack of antlers   how precarious and how quickly
he would soon melt away into   the liquefying night

*

I was speaking of a bird
as if it were a microcosm
a generality
a supernumerary

then moments
later a hawk lunged
for a chickadee

on the back deck

Day 18

The reference point   is not   the vanishing point
it is stable   it is as permanent as I   am
which isn't very   except that it will last as long as I do
after which   yes   the vanishing point

*

Scrap of ground

where I would sit
day after long day

neither a songbird

nor a student
of the wind

Day 46

The apples had been   left   on the tree   through October
through the soft and heavy frosts   into November
shriveled and shrunk   until it was   necessary
that they fall   and then not only   the deer   with their long
necks but the rabbits   with their short legs   could eat

*

Whereon is a word no
one uses anymore
we have no need

for precise placement
of people places
things and ideas

sometimes I feel despair
that language is used to consume
and deplete

Day 80

Solstice daylight leaching away into dark   time to
light the fire already laid   in the fireplace
glory these flames   that make the winter dark   less bitter

Gratitude is supposed to hurt   I say   while you stand
with your hands on your heart   wrinkling up your face
and the fire   flares up   and the days pass   each shorter than the one
before   and now a little snow is falling sideways   across the field
turning everything

*

We didn't come here
we were never
present

we were not
able to be

and the place
sails on without
us

Day with a self in it

An empty space one day
the next another

long strip of beach
with the sound

rolling in
and out

A white house with windows
in the east

a house
without

a cellar
or any way down

A ground full
of red clover

and a scattering
of bees

a mown empty
field

A rusty pump handle
in the woods

What you said to me
so long ago

that I remember
or do I not

A gush of rain

A winter without windows
house without a door

A wind that keeps
the little things together

keeps the words
from falling into

a long white space

Little things
perfect circles

with black centers
and you

walking at the edge

Day 96

And what of all   the people who love   to see birds
who write down the date and time   they sight   each species
I think it is about   beholding   the world
and do you think   it will have been enough

*

A shift in the way
time
travels
unravels

Day 97

Here I am and   here you are
not: that is how survivorship   shall be
the long gap between   us
diminished only   by my mind   and what
it can hold   of you   of us   for the remainder

*

We have wanted
other
always other
as time chips away
at words and what they stand for
as time fills the spaces between with its species
we have wanted and wanted
what time takes away

Day 106

The moon centimetering   away   at the rate of two
each year   and it will take millions
or maybe billions of years but eventually the moon
will break   free of Earth and orbit the sun
(in all-engulfing nova)   on its own   we will be
long gone   by then   we humans
who like to think   that the world began
with us   and will never   come to an end
because we are unable   to imagine our own

*

A few knots of dry leaves
          sticking to the bare trees
               like little brown ornaments
                    twinkling in late sun and snow
                         skein of geese knitting the sky
                              I see so much farther now

Day 156

After a long and brutal   February I am
ready to assert   spring
I want to   avenge all the life that winter
takes away with its fierce   pitilessness

*

This cold
this bright
this white
this day
full of
birdsong
and wind
the possible
probable
end to
winter
or to what
I believe

The loneliness of a planet without a moon

I went out at dayrise
before the sun

and because it was spring
the birds had already

begun

it was hard to tell if I had not known
whether it was the verge of morning or of night

but we don't have words for the morning dusk
the gloaming
twilight

because we are not so often there

but I saw the moon
early

its edges fading
into the morning

Day 166

Have you been saved   is an intimate most personal
question I don't want   to answer or in fact
to be asked   most things have been   saved at least once
in their existence: a bird   by shadow from a kestrel
a rock from a hard   fall from a cliffs edge
a man with a gun   at his back by
another soldier   behind the other
a moon from complete   darkness by the angle
of the sun   a child crossing   the road by good brakes
a word fallen into disuse   by one who mines   old dictionaries for
their riches   me by you

*

I like to see
what's survived
the winter
what comes up
green one
more time

Day 186

The days fall away   or speed by   or sink
and they are all gone so soon—surprise!—
What gets left   behind the days
Just memory   and a few   questions   but for my friend
with no past   nothing
and I think we are just   the sum   of what   we can recall

*

No particular day

Day 227

The days can no longer   hold their disguises   and must
appear as they are   without the figments
of another imagination

*

Give up on naming the days
they have their own nomenclature

Release the May-blooming trees
they have their own timetable

And allow the sound of birds
to come and go as they will

For you have no control
and must let go

Day 269

A bit of rain   after a long   dry spell
as if drought is a form   of magic
that holds life in   suspension

I think of the Rainy River   and the time I spent in it
often among raindrops—   in the river
the river in me   still cold   at the solstice
not really warm enough to swim in until   July
and meanwhile on our little planet we turn—   not the sun
which is   impervious   to its satellites
and their satellites   and answers the call of another

*

I love how it comes toward me
as if to embrace

Day 274

If you get too close   to the sun   you will have no moon
no moon at all: Venus perhaps   your moon has burned up
in the general conflagration   of Mercury or maybe
your moon has fled   to cooler climes   even little cold Pluto
has a bitty moon   but Jupiter and Saturn
have taken more   than their share

We here have only one   but it saves us
from so much sorrow

*

Home is a yellow leaf that sails the wind
a wood shack in a green wood
the tails side of a shiny dime
the signature on a letter
the place beside the old house where I buried my first dog
the stack of sheet music on the piano
that I can't play any more
the dust of stars

Day 299

How many moons are enough?   Saturn
has a surfeit of moons   by my standards   which is to say
from the point of view of Earth   tides are all about   attraction
Newton said and he was   often right   but not always
an apple falls   the moon pulls   its weight while the sun
forces the issue   but what of Saturn   where the moons number seventy-
odd   do they exert force on   or can the giant ignore them
Enceladus the ice moon   with a liquid interior   in a landscape close to
absolute zero   the sun a distant clot

Perhaps the nearer planets   want no moons   close
as they are to the sun   and those farther away
need something to comfort them

*

Oh what does it all mean we humans ask
as far as we know
we're the only ones who insist on meaning

the fractures open like a fist unclenching
divulging the interior's intense heat

I sometimes need that kind of comfort

Day 307

Now we have turned once more   away from the sun
inching back   toward the indistinguishable   dark

*

Mercury who has
stolen your moons?
A fiery beast
come too near

Day 314

I love graveyards   how quiet   they are
the wind sluicing through   the granite
and marble stones   a tree here and   there
I say hello   to my ancestors   three generations
lying side by side   and trim
the giant crabapple   I planted   twenty-eight years ago
to shade my father   I won't be buried here   instead
I'll fly to the four winds   and the eight waters
and the sky!   Oh yes
the sky

*

Ah Mother you made me
dig deep

Day 315

The moon's pull   the tides   of inland lakes
are sometimes too subtle   to notice
the spring tide on   Lake Superior
might rise   just two inches

Have you seen it—   the tiny ripple   along the shoreline
and what it leaves   behind
a thin layer   of water weed   green until the sun bleaches it
and the next wind   arrives

The moon a   failure   in the smallest pond
except in reflection

*

My body this strange
and brilliant being

Day 321

Getting up later   but still in night
is the way darkness gets   the better of light

*

The leaves are still
green but not
that green
the one
with which it all begins

so we are moving
toward the end
once again

Day 344

And then   after a scattering   of drops
we got rain   it finally rained
there is a strong smell of ozone in the air   and flowers
some late-summer   wild bloom that I can't   identify
but recognize from   time ago

*

Wood all around with knotted marks
an upturned boat
or something carved
from a crow's call

incense drifting across the hull
fragments of color from stained glass
alighting randomly
no oars or oarlocks

the boat is self-propelled
the priest a ragged voice
the crows are praying in the rain
outside the individual

drops and the individual leaves
speak to one another
and ignore us all
we kneel upside down

and say amen because that
is how it always ends

Day with a notion in it

Things have to restart regularly
to stay on track

even lives

I'm watching the saints
finish up their earthly beings

so many of them
are like so many others

it's hard to keep them
apart

and everything else I see
I am pretty sure

I've seen before

the way the leaves
shrivel
before they fall

the flash of marigold
on the branch

people who throw
garbage
out of their cars

on my sweet little backwater street
and this summer

the slough has gone
completely dry

I know I've seen
a drought like this

at least once before

but I tried to forget it
and succeeded

until now

and the scattered sticks
and broken things

and people limping
by on crutches

and the ones
whose childhoods

make me believe
in reincarnation

if only I could pick
the right word

from the list or
even better find it

where there are none
to choose from

if only my notion
of you could match up

with the real you

Day 350

Parts of me travel   more slowly than others
and I have to wait   for them to catch up
in the meantime   I must be patient   and live
in the hollows   and interstices

You might call it   hallowed ground   this place where
nothing is complete   and nothing can be
saved

*

Little nothings and big
nothings vie for space

among the ordinary

Day 351

Thin   the lost things   so thin they lose a dimension
here they are   the numbers say   they are here   but unknown
so quickly   we emerge   from the great   unconscious
and so swiftly   we return

*

Swifts with their scissor tails
and highly aerial wings
can sleep while they fly

and belong with the hummingbirds
and the godwits

What kind of intelligence
places these two together
what kind of mind orders them

Swifts can stay airborne for ten months

*

The natural darkness that precedes it

Day 358

Watching the coffee eddy as   I agitate and
it drains   through the filter   I think perhaps
the universe with its swirling   galaxies is being
lightly shaken

*

I want to play Dvorak
on the piano but
there are too many
flats

*

I can't think in flats

*

But I can listen in flats

*

When
the end is becoming
visible

*

The arrow is pointing southeast
that's where the sun
comes from now
just before
the equinox going toward winter

Day 361

What direction does light come from
and where is it going

What direction is the sun heading in
and when will it arrive

Is there any somewhere
in a universe
with two billion
give or take
galaxies

or is it all

*

I have questions
and no one has answers

*

I have questions
for which
there are no answers

*

I have questions
that no one answers

*

I have no one's questions

*

The wind this afternoon
the wind wants to
take things away

if the wind has desire
which I tend to
think it has

I know that rocks do
so why not the wind

*

I should go back
to where I was before
all this

*

if back is anywhere

*

I see greenly now
but soon
I will see
more sky

*

That means it's fall

*

and a leaf here and there

*

begins to burn

Kathleen Jesme is the author of five previous collections of poetry: *Albedo* and *The Plum-Stone Game* from Ahsahta Press; *Meridian*, winner of the Snowbound Chapbook Prize from Tupelo Press; *Motherhouse*, winner of the Lena-Miles Wever Todd Poetry Prize from Pleiades Press; and *Fire Eater*, from the University of Tampa Press. She holds a Master of Fine Arts degree from Warren Wilson College.